THOMAS CRANE PUBLIC LIBRARY
QUINCY MA

CITY APPROPRIATION

Life in the Early Islamic World

Arts and Culture
in the Early Islamic World

Lizann Flatt

Crabtree Publishing Company
www.crabtreebooks.com

Life in the Early Islamic World

Author: Lizann Flatt
Publishing plan research and development:
    Sean Charlebois, Reagan Miller
    Crabtree Publishing Company
Editor-in-Chief: Lionel Bender
Editors: Simon Adams, Lynn Peppas
Proofreaders: Laura Booth, Wendy Scavuzzo
Editorial director: Kathy Middleton
Design and photo research: Ben White
Production: Kim Richardson
Prepress technician: Katherine Berti
Print and production coordinator:
    Katherine Berti

Consultants:
    Barbara Petzen, Education Director,
    Middle East Policy Council and President,
    Middle East Outreach Council;

    Brian Williams, B.A., Educational
    Publishing Consultant and Editor.

Cover: Antique ottoman seamless wallpaper
    (background); Ancient Islamic Tower (center);
    ottoman hammam bowl (bottom left); a page
    from the story *Kelileh o Demneh* (bottom right)
Title page: Calligraphic Lion

Photographs and reproductions:
The Art Archive: 16 (Bibliothèque des Arts Décoratifs
    Paris/Gianni Dagli Orti), 18 (Gianni Dagli Orti), 21
    (Musée du Louvre Paris/Gianni Dagli Orti), 22 (Topkapi
    Museum Istanbul/Gianni Dagli Orti), 25 (Victoria and
    Albert Museum London/V&A Images), 27 (Musée du
    Louvre Paris/Gianni Dagli Orti), 28 (Musée du Louvre
    Paris/Gianni Dagli Orti), 30 (British Library), 35 (The
    Granger Collection), 36 (Kharbine-Tapabor/Collection
    MX), 39 (Topkapi Library Istanbul/Gianni Dagli Orti),
    43 (Topkapi Library Istanbul/Gianni Dagli Orti)
shutterstock.com: cover-bottom left (gezik), 1 (Lawrence
    Wee), 3 (Vladimir Melnik) (4–5 (Artography), 6
    (Ahmad Fayzal Yahya), 8–9 (Goran Bogicevic), 9 (Sufi),
    13 (mypokcik), 15t, 15b (Ahmad Fayzal Yahya), 16–17
    (rm), 18 (Galyna Andrushko), 20–21 (sano7), 23 (Clara),
    24 (Circumnavigation), 29 (Zurijeta), 31 (Rechitan Sorin),
    37 (cenap refik ongan).
Thinkstock: cover-center (iStockphoto)
Topfoto (The Granger Collection): 12–13, 38; 10–11 (HIP),
    11 (The Image Works), 26 (The British Library/HIP), 33
    (Ullsteinbild), 40–41 The British Library/HIP).
Wikimedia Commons: cover-bottom right (Zereshk)

Maps:
Stefan Chabluk

This book was produced for Crabtree Publishing
Company by Bender Richardson White.

Library and Archives Canada Cataloguing in Publication

Flatt, Lizann
    Arts and culture in the early Islamic world / Lizann Flatt.

(Life in the early Islamic world)
Includes index.
Issued also in electronic formats.
ISBN 978-0-7787-2167-3 (bound).--ISBN 978-0-7787-2174-1 (pbk.)

    1. Islamic art--History--Juvenile literature. I. Title. II. Series: Life
in the early Islamic world

N6260.F53 2012   j709.17'67   C2012-900273-9

Library of Congress Cataloging-in-Publication Data

Flatt, Lizann.
    Arts and culture in the early Islamic world / Lizann Flatt.
      p. cm. -- (Life in the early Islamic world)
    Includes index.
    ISBN 978-0-7787-2167-3 (reinforced library binding : alk. paper) --
    ISBN 978-0-7787-2174-1 (pbk. : alk. paper) -- ISBN 978-1-4271-9837-2
    (electronic pdf) -- ISBN 978-1-4271-9560-9 (electronic html)
    1. Islamic art--Juvenile literature. I. Title.

    N6260.F53 2012
    700.917'67--dc23
                                                    2012000074

Crabtree Publishing Company

www.crabtreebooks.com   1-800-387-7650

Printed in Canada/022012/AV20120110

Published in Canada
Crabtree Publishing
616 Welland Ave.
St. Catharines, Ontario
L2M 5V6

Published in the United States
Crabtree Publishing
PMB 59051
350 Fifth Avenue, 59th Floor
New York, New York 10118

Published in the United Kingdom
Crabtree Publishing
Maritime House
Basin Road North, Hove
BN41 1WR

Published in Australia
Crabtree Publishing
3 Charles Street
Coburg North
VIC, 3058

Contents

IN THE BEGINNING	4	CARPETS	28
CALLIGRAPHY	8	TEXTILES AND LEATHER	30
ARCHITECTURE	12	BOOKS	32
MOSQUES	14	POETRY AND PROSE	34
PALACES AND HOMES	16	MUSIC AND DANCE	36
TOMBS, MADRASAS,		PAINTING	40
AND INNS	18	Biographies	42
CARVINGS	20	Timelines	44
POTTERY	22	Glossary	46
GLASSWARE	24	Further Information	47
METALWARE	26	Index	48

About This Book

Islam is the religion of Muslim people. Muslims believe in one God. They believe that the prophet Muhammad is the messenger of God. Islam began in the early 600s C.E. in the Arabian peninsula, in a region that is now the country of Saudi Arabia. From there, it spread across the world. Today, there are about 1.5 billion Muslims. About half of all Muslims live in southern Asia. Many Muslims also live in the Middle East and Africa, with fewer in Europe, North America, and Australia.

Arts and Culture in the Early Islamic World looks at how Islamic designs, styles, and craft skills developed and how these were used in and influenced architecture, decoration, household objects, written materials, music, and illustration. Many of the historic arts and cultural influences can be seen today.

In the Beginning

Islam **is a religion. It was founded by the** prophet **Muhammad, who lived from 570 to 632** C.E. **From its start in Arabia, Islam spread quickly throughout the Middle East, parts of Asia, and North Africa. The followers of the religion**—Muslims—**shared the same beliefs and evolved unique styles of art and architecture.**

Decorative Art

Much Islamic art is "decorative," which means it is useful as well as beautiful, such as a painted pot, an illustrated book, or a carved table. "Fine" art, such as a painting, has no such everyday use. In the Islamic world, decorative art included glassware, **ceramics**, carvings, **textiles**, metalwork, tilework, and carpets. Artists learned both techniques and styles of decoration from older **cultures**, such as the **Sasanian** and **Byzantine** empires.

Styles of art varied at different times and places within the Islamic world. They also changed as the Islamic Empire expanded and foreign influences took effect. Yet Islamic art kept some qualities and rules. The main features were **arabesque**, or stylized plant patterns, as well as geometric shapes, and decorative lettering or **calligraphy**.

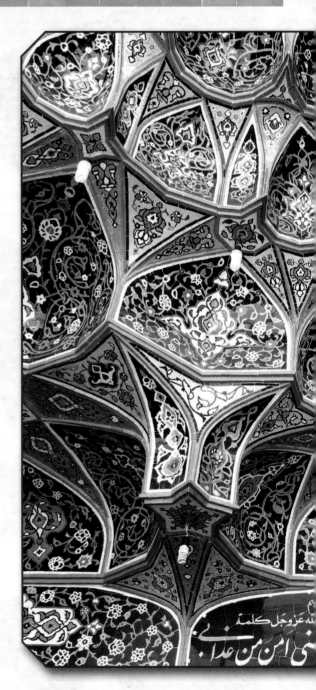

Below: **Muqarnas** are three-dimensional, decorated features found on the ceilings of many Islamic buildings. They look like the stalactites found in caves.

Islamic Art

Islam affects everything its followers do, including art and design. Muslims have formed a distinct Islamic style of art. Not all Islamic art, however, was made for religious purposes. Different regions had their own styles. These were influenced by local customs, traditions, and ways of life.

Islamic Timeline

570–632 Muhammad's lifetime
632–661 Rule of the first four **caliphs**
661–750 Umayyad **Dynasty**
711 Start of Islamic conquest of Spain and Portugal
750–1258 Abbasid Dynasty
909–1171 Fatimid rulers in North Africa, Egypt, and Syria
1050–1147 Almoravids rule North Africa and Spain
1071 Seljuk Turks defeat the Byzantines
1096 First Christian Crusade begins against Islamic rule in the Holy Land of Palestine
1169–1250 Ayyubids rule Egypt and Syria (Saladin is their most famous ruler)
1250–1517 Mamluks rule Egypt and Syria
1370–1507 Timurid Dynasty in Iran
1501–1736 Safavids rule Iran
1526–1857 **Mughal** Empire in India
1517–1918 **Ottoman** Empire

Islamic Art

Islamic art often used the arabesque patterns in decoration. Artists liked to repeat interlaced or scroll patterns, often covering surfaces to make an intricate design. The patterns were mostly made of flowers or leaves in a "nonreal" way. In other words, the flowers and leaves were not drawn from nature, but in a graphic way. These patterns were used on books, buildings, textiles, and household objects.

Tessellation is another element of Islamic art. This is the use of a repeated shape or several shapes with no overlap and no gaps. Geometric patterns were based on circles, squares, stars, triangles, and other shapes. The shapes were joined, interlaced, and repeated to make complex designs. Calligraphy was also used to make patterns. Often, arabesque, tessellation, geometric patterns, and calligraphy were used together.

Another important point about Islamic art—and one that makes it different from most other art in the world—is that artists tried not to show pictures of people or animals in religious settings. Figures were left out because most Muslims believed that making images of people or animals could lead to **idolatory**, or the worship of images.

Artists showed animals or people in nonreligious art. The **miniatures** painted on **manuscripts**, or handwritten texts, were meant to help people understand

Craftworkers

Craftworkers, such as **smiths**, formed guilds, or groups. Guilds were important in Islamic society. Workers with special skills included blacksmiths, goldsmiths, and even performers. Members helped one another to support the guild. The guilds were sometimes so strong they could stand against the government.

Above: The **Kaaba** in Mecca—the most holy site for all Muslims—is covered with a cloth decorated with gold calligraphy.

the words, so animals or people were often shown. **Persian** art, for example, was rich in miniature painting. Figures were also shown on textiles and decorative objects. Sculptures, like those in Greek or Chinese art, are rare in Islamic art.

The Islamic Empire

This map shows how far the early Islamic Empire had reached by about 750 C.E. Islam had begun in the towns of Mecca and Medina in 622, then spread quickly across the rest of Arabia. Muslim armies then took Islam to many distant lands. Parts of the Byzantine Empire in Western Asia and North Africa were conquered, along with the Sasanian or Persian Empire to the east.

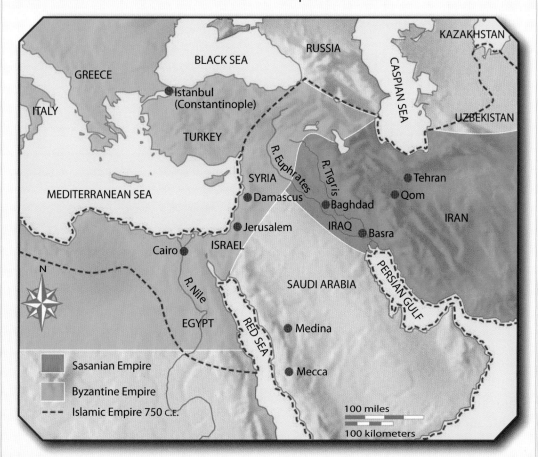

The map highlights some of the many cities that became important Islamic centers of art and culture. Modern city and country names are used. There was a great deal of exchange of ideas and techniques between these centers. Travelers from other parts of Europe and Asia brought in new styles of design.

Calligraphy

Calligraphy is the art of decorative writing. Many people think it is the highest art form in the Islamic world. Calligraphy uses Arabic script as art. Words can be written in different styles of lettering.

What is Calligraphy

In calligraphy, letters are made to look beautiful, so words become art. Words written in Arabic script remind people of the **Quran**, the holy book of Islam that contains the messages Muhammad had brought from Allah, or God. Without calligraphy, people might worship the picture of a person or even an animal as an idol and not remember God's message.

Calligraphy was used in different materials on different objects. It appeared on weapons, tools, buildings, jewelry, textiles, and also on paintings and books. Decorative letters and words were carved in wood, traced in plaster, and painted on ceramics such as tiles. In a **mosque**—the Muslim house of worship—calligraphy usually consisted of verses from the Quran or carefully chosen words from religious teachers. On nonreligious buildings, calligraphy might be poetry, names, or dates. In early Islamic history, coins were often stamped with calligraphy, not the picture of a ruler.

Arabic Script

The Arabic alphabet has 28 basic letters. There are 17 distinct letter forms or shapes. The other 11 letter forms are made by adding dots above or below the main shapes to indicate sounds. Diagonal strokes stand for short vowel sounds. Arabic script is written and read from right to left.

Sign of the Sultan

The **sultans** who ruled the Ottoman Empire had a special handwritten seal or personal mark as a sign of their power. Called a *tughra*, it looked like a fancy signature. Each sultan had his own design. The tughra was added by **scribes** to official papers to show they came from the sultan. A tughra, rather than the sultan's picture, was also put on coins. A tughra was made up of the sultan's name, his father's name, his title, and the words "ever victorious."

Above: This tughra in mosaic—small pieces of colored stone, glass, or ceramics—is a sultan's sign. It was made up at the beginning of a sultan's rule by the court calligrapher.

Left: This closeup shows how beautiful ornate Islamic calligraphy can look when carved in stone. Arabesque vines spiral in the background.

Calligraphic Styles

Different styles of calligraphy appeared over the centuries. The first form was *kufic*. The first Qurans were written in this script. In the kufic script, letter forms are squared. Calligraphers then produced more decorative flowing scripts over time. During the 900s, calligraphers made rules for word and letter spacing, and for letter forms. Each of the six main scripts, or ways of writing, in Arabic has its own rules. The six scripts are called the Six Pens.

Pens and Paper

A *qalam* or reed pen was the usual writing tool, although brushes were also used. Pens were valuable **trade** items throughout the Islamic world. A calligrapher cut a qalam from a reed, a lakeside plant. The sharp tip was dipped in ink. Ink colors were black, brown, blue, red, yellow, white, silver, and gold. Making ink was complicated and took days. The make-up of some ink colors were guarded secrets. Soot, gall nuts, and henna were among the ingredients used to make various colors.

Calligraphy was first written on parchment, a material made from dried animal skins. Papyrus—a type of paper made from reeds in Egypt—was also used. Papermaking was first learned from China in 751. Paper was made from silk, or plant fibers such as cotton.

Paper was cheaper, easier to cut, and took color better than other writing materials. As it became more available, paper advanced the art of calligraphy.

The calligrapher or scribe was an important person in Islamic society. Many scribes acted as secretaries to rulers and governments. Others worked for scholars; qadis, or judges; imams, who led prayers at

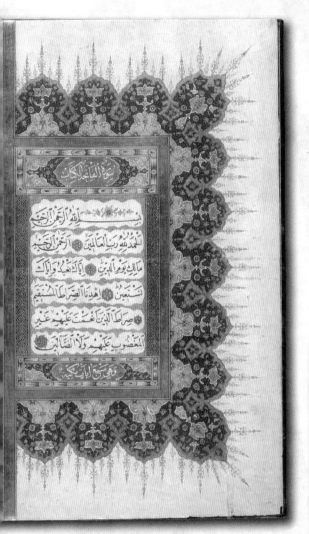

Above: Pages from the Quran show Arabic calligraphy with decorations in the margins.

Ibn Muqlah

Ibn Muqlah (886–940) made rules for calligraphic letters. He based his rules on the diamond-shaped dot a reed pen makes on paper. Using these dots, he worked out the height of *alif,* the first letter of the Arabic alphabet. Then he found the size of the other letters compared to the alif. In this way, he invented "proportioned" script, in which all the letters are related in size. He was one of the greatest Islamic calligraphers.

the mosques; and other important people. A scribe worked at a desk, but sometimes he sat on the ground, with one leg folded under his body and the other leg bent. He held the paper on his knee supported by his left palm or a piece of **pasteboard**. He wore at his waist a case for writing materials.

Above: A young boy writes on a board Arabic calligraphy for prayers. Note that he writes from right to left.

Architecture

The peoples within the Islamic world had different cultures, and architecture varied from place to place and also changed through time. Some features were shared: open spaces; use of natural light; fountains; tiles; calligraphic decoration; and decorated ceilings.

Space and Light

Islamic architecture focused on the use of inner space. Many buildings had an open inner courtyard to allow space for people to gather. The courtyard was usually surrounded by rooms or by an arcade, which is a roofed walkway that gave shelter from the hot wind and sun. An inner courtyard also let cool night air into the building. Symmetry, or a balanced design, was not as important in Islamic as it was in European architecture, so some buildings had extensions built onto the courtyard at the side. All buildings were designed to let in plenty of natural light.

Many Muslims lived in hot, dry lands. Water was precious and a symbol of Paradise, so water became an important feature of Islamic architecture. There was often a fountain or pool in the central courtyard to provide both beauty and coolness. In a mosque, people used water to wash before prayers.

Other typical features were tall towers called **minarets**, from which the call to prayer was given by an appointed person; and large domes, and *iwans*. An iwan is a large hall or open space with walls on three sides, often opening onto the central courtyard.

Domes or arches were highly decorated. Muqarnas were common on ceilings. Rather similar was the *mocárabe*, a form of decoration that looks like stalactites or honeycombs, that was used on windows, arches, and columns. Decorative elements outside and inside buildings included calligraphy and brightly colored tiles.

Right: Carved and highly decorated arches, a marble floor, and a fountain can be seen in this building in Morocco.

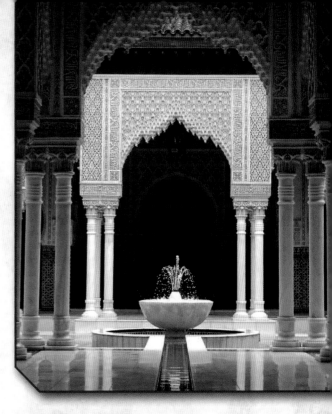

The Bazaar

Bazaars are markets where people trade goods and services. They are common across the Islamic world. From early times, every city had a bazaar. Often located in narrow streets, the bazaar had a canvas or wooden covering to protect people from the weather. Each section of the bazaar sold a specific type of good, such as spices, fabric, carpets, metal and leather goods, pottery, jewelry, or foods. Bazaars often included coffee houses, restaurants, and inns, and were usually built near a mosque, which people visited every day.

Below: This painting from a Turkish manuscript shows a bazaar. There are stalls for a jeweler, pharmacist, butcher, and baker.

Mosques

The mosque is the most important building in an Islamic community. Worshipers come to the mosque daily to pray. Friday prayers are especially important. On one wall, there is often a niche to show that this wall is nearest to Mecca. Most mosques have a courtyard and high minarets, or towers. There are three main styles of mosque: open-plan, four-iwan, and domed.

Three Styles

The open-plan mosque has a central courtyard surrounded by arcades, with minarets on top of the building. Such mosques are found around the Mediterranean region. Examples are the mosques of Damascus and Córdoba.

The four-iwan mosque has four hallways or iwans that lead out from a central courtyard. Its minarets are often set lower down on the building. Pre-Islamic Sasanid architecture influenced the four-iwan style of mosque, which is found in Iran and Central Asia.

The domed mosque was a feature of the Ottoman Empire. Domed mosques have huge open spaces beneath these rounded roofs. They also have columns and, on the roof, cupolas, or small domes. The Sultan Ahmet Mosque is an example.

Although these are different styles of mosques, all feature a courtyard—an open space for worshipers to gather. All have a covered space for prayers and a *qibla* wall to mark the side of the mosque closest to Mecca. A decorated niche or arch, called a *mihrab*, is often located in the qibla wall. These features also appear in modern mosques built in contemporary styles.

Important Mosques

After the al-Haram Mosque in Mecca (see below), the Masjid al-Nabawi, or Prophet's Mosque, in Medina is the most important.

The Kaaba

The holiest mosque in the Islamic world is the al-Haram Mosque in Mecca. It is built around the Kaaba— a cube-shaped structure of granite blocks. Some people believe that the ancient black stone that lies embedded in its eastern corner is a meteorite. The Kaaba is the most holy site in Islam and is covered by a black cloth embroidered with gold calligraphy. Muslims pray facing the direction of the Kaaba. The Kaaba has been destroyed and rebuilt many times over the centuries. All Muslims who can afford it go on a **pilgrimage** to the Kaaba at least once in their life.

Right: The Sultan Ahmet Mosque, built between 1609 and 1616, dominates the skyline of Constantinople (now Istanbul) in Turkey.

Below: In Medina, Saudi Arabia, Muslims study and discuss the Quran inside the Masjid al-Nabawi. This is known as the Prophet's Mosque.

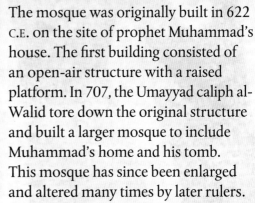

The mosque was originally built in 622 C.E. on the site of prophet Muhammad's house. The first building consisted of an open-air structure with a raised platform. In 707, the Umayyad caliph al-Walid tore down the original structure and built a larger mosque to include Muhammad's home and his tomb. This mosque has since been enlarged and altered many times by later rulers.

Islam's third most holy mosque is the al-Aqsa in Jerusalem. It stands beside another religious building, the Dome of the Rock. The Dome of the Rock is an important shrine for pilgrims. It stands on the spot from which Muslims believe Muhammad went on his Night Journey. It has a gold dome and is covered in colorful ceramic tiles. It was built by Caliph Abd al-Malik from 689 to 691.

Palaces and Homes

Many Muslims lived in cities protected by moats, thick walls, large gates, and towers. These cities were built from local materials such as stone or unbaked bricks. A ruler lived in a fortress or fortified palace and moved house as the seasons changed.

Palaces

A palace was a ruler's home, as well as a place of government. Generally, the outer areas of a palace housed government offices, a mint for making coins, and a weapons' store. There were also kitchens, stables, and a hall where the ruler met his officials. The private living areas were at the center of the palace and included halls for private meetings, family areas, libraries, and treasuries for valuables.

Left: This painted scene of a summer house in Iraq shows how rulers and rich people enjoyed getting away from the city, especially in the heat of summer.

The Alhambra Palace in Granada, Spain, is one of the most famous Islamic palaces. An example of **Moorish** design, it was built in the 1300s. Several rulers added to the "red house," which in Arabic is *al-Hamra*. The outside of the palace is quite plain, but inside are beautiful courtyards, arcades, halls, rooms, baths, fountains, and pools. The site is known for the red-and-white arches that decorate the inside. The palace complex has maze-like gardens. The Alhambra ceased to be a Muslim palace with the Christian conquest of Granada in 1492.

Islamic Homes

Houses were designed to suit the local environment and culture. In many urban areas, homes of the rich had high walls for privacy and security. A shared entrance from a single door led to a hallway off which individual rooms could be visited. Gardens and courtyards for the family to enjoy were integral parts. In the hot, arid Middle East, there were often fountains and windtowers to help keep the buildings cool. Most Muslim homes had a separate section for the owner's family, where women of the household had privacy from guests and visitors.

An Air-Conditioning System

In desert conditions, buildings needed to be kept cool. One way to do this was to construct a windtower. Shutters at the top of the tower caught the wind, drawing air down into the building. Ducts and airways inside allowed the cool air to circulate, then be drawn out of the building.

Above: Work started on the Topkapi Palace in Constantinople (now Istanbul) in 1459. It was the home of the Ottoman sultans for about 400 years.

Tombs, Madrasas, and Inns

Schools, inns, and bathhouses were just some of the Islamic buildings that had architectural features in common. So too did special buildings for the dead.

Mausoleums

Mausoleums were built over and around burial places. These buildings were treated as monuments. Like other Islamic buildings, many of them had domes and decorations. Some even rivaled palaces in their splendor. The Taj Mahal in Agra, India, is among the most famous of mausoleums. This beautiful building was built by the Mughal emperor Shah Jahan, for his favorite wife, Mumtaz Mahal.

Madrasas

Muslims went to the mosque to pray. Over time, specialized schools called *madrasas* were built next to them to instruct students in Arabic, Islamic law, and religious teachings. Rulers and wealthy citizens paid for teachers and other staff, scholarships for students, and building repairs. A madrasa included living quarters for the teacher and some students. The first known madrasa was set up in Egypt in 1005. The buildings shared features of other Islamic buildings, such as courtyards, minarets, and iwans.

Below: The Taj Mahal in India is the world's most famous mausoleum. Built between 1632 and 1653 for an Islamic emperor's dead wife, it is clad in white marble.

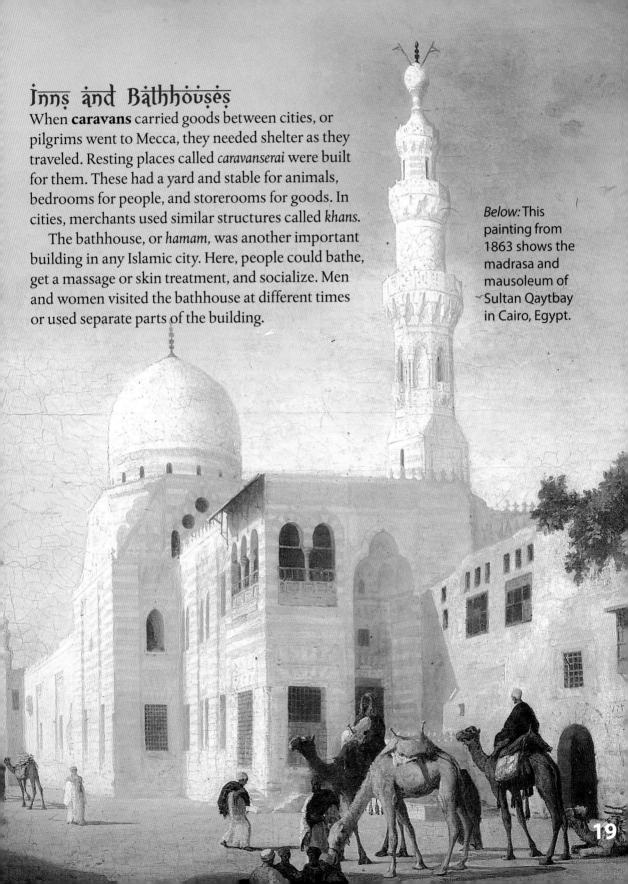

Inns and Bathhouses

When **caravans** carried goods between cities, or pilgrims went to Mecca, they needed shelter as they traveled. Resting places called *caravanserai* were built for them. These had a yard and stable for animals, bedrooms for people, and storerooms for goods. In cities, merchants used similar structures called *khans*.

The bathhouse, or *hamam*, was another important building in any Islamic city. Here, people could bathe, get a massage or skin treatment, and socialize. Men and women visited the bathhouse at different times or used separate parts of the building.

Below: This painting from 1863 shows the madrasa and mausoleum of Sultan Qaytbay in Cairo, Egypt.

19

Carvings

Elaborate carving in wood, stone, plaster, and ivory was used to decorate surfaces large and small.

Raw Materials

As well as being used for structural parts, such as roofs and beams, wood was used for decoration in buildings. It was carved in intricate patterns for doors, boxes, ceilings, and panels. Wood was also used for Quran stands, prayer niches, and game boards. Wooden doors were carved and inlaid with carved bone or ivory. Wood was also carved and plastered, then painted, to make the decorative features on ceilings.

A *minbar*, made of wood or stone, was a feature of many mosques. This was like a staircase of eight to 12 steps. From the top, a preacher could be heard by everyone in the mosque. The minbar was often elaborately carved.

Right: This detailed plaster carving shows plants in an arabesque style that is typical of Islamic art.

Mudejar Craftsmen

After Christian armies reconquered Spain in the late 1400s, some Muslims remained. They were first allowed to keep their Islamic faith, but were eventually forced to convert or leave. These Spanish Muslims were called *mudejar*. Many were skilled artists, especially in woodwork. They made fine ceilings decorated with interlacing geometric patterns, and doors and furniture that were beautifully carved and painted. Other mudejar were skilled potters, metalworkers, and weavers. Their work shaped the art and architecture of much of Spain.

Arabesque patterns were cut into the stones of domes and arched doorways of mosques in Egypt. Carved or pierced screens made from red sandstone were used in Mughal India for window openings and room dividers. Such screens cut out glare from the sun and let in a cooling breeze. Ivory was used in finely carved round boxes, hunting horns, and on window screens. Carved ivory panels were often set into wooden furniture such as tables.

Left: This *pyx*, or casket, is made of engraved elephant ivory, with the name al-Mughira carved in calligraphy. It is dated 968.

Pottery

Pottery and ceramics were made from clay baked at extremely high temperatures in ovens called kilns. Ceramics ranged from useful pots and bowls to beautiful tiles on mosque walls and other buildings.

Everyday Use

The range of Islamic pottery produced included dishes, bowls, platters, jugs, and jars for storing and transporting oil, grain, and water. Lamps used in mosques were also made from pottery. Unglazed pottery, or earthenware, was made for the kitchen and general use, including shops. Glazed ceramics were objects of great beauty and were traded for a high price.

Right: An Iznik water bottle, made around 1570. Iznik ware potters used vivid purple, red, and green colors, as well as blue.

Imitating China

The Turkish city of Iznik became known for a highly decorated type of pottery and tiles. Iznik pottery was made by painting a hard, white ceramic and then adding a clear lead glaze. Blue and white designs were particularly popular. These imitated and adapted the style of Chinese **porcelain** that itself had been influenced by designs from Iraq.

Below: These colorful ceramic tiles are of Ottoman design and come from Constantinople (now Istanbul).

Clays and Glazes

During the Abbasid Dynasty, Islamic potters tried to copy the highly prized white porcelain from China. They experimented with different glazes and clays. They mixed crushed glass, quartz sand, and clay to make a hard, white ceramic called fritware or stonepaste. Glazes that, when fired, produced an opaque or nontransparent white finish were useful, since they formed a good surface to decorate.

Slip-painting pottery was another technique that was used. Thin liquid-like clay, or slip, was applied over earthenware. A white slip pot could be painted in many colors. Often the slip was cut to a design, then glazed or painted to give it an extra finish.

Lusterware was also made by Abbasid potters. In this method, pigments made from silver or copper were painted in intricate designs onto glazed ceramics. The ceramics were then specially fired or heated. The result was items that shone as if they were made of gold or silver.

During the 1000s, Seljuk Empire potters made Minai ware, also known as enameled ware. The potter applied more colored pigments over a glazed fritware pot. The pot was then fired again, but at a lower temperature. This resulted in vibrantly colorful works.

Glassware

Islamic glass was both useful and decorative. Early local expertise in glassmaking was adapted to create distinct Islamic styles. Glassware from the Middle East was highly prized, particularly in China.

New Techniques

Many items were made by blowing air through a tube into a ball of molten glass to create a bubble that was twisted and turned. Most everyday glass objects were plain and undecorated. Special items used by the rich were highly decorated. Everyday items were made quickly and cheaply. Glass was also put into molds to create different shapes.

Rock Crystal

During the Fatimid Dynasty, craftworkers carved chunks of clear quartz known as rock crystal. This looked like glass and was used to make jugs, vessels, and bottles. Such objects were prized by people at the ruler's court. Some of these rock crystal pieces were traded across Europe, where they were used in Christian churches as containers for holy remains.

Above: Colored glass was used to make beautiful windows. The formulas to make some colors of glass were kept secret.

Above left: This Egyptian mosque lamp was made from gilded and enameled, or colored, glass during the mid-1300s.

Glassmakers decorated glass in various ways. One method was to apply glass threads or trails over the surface. Another was to cut into the cold, hard glass with cutting stones or small wheels to make complicated honeycomb patterns. Two layers of differently colored glass were also used. Relief-cut glass was made by cutting and grinding away the unwanted glass from around the design, leaving a raised decoration.

Luster-painted glass became popular from the 600s to the 800s. This was made by first putting silver or copper pigment onto the glass, and then firing the object. The result was a metallic sheen on the glass. The same technique was also used for ceramics. Gilded glass was made by applying molten liquid gold to a glass object. The object was then fired at a low temperature to fuse the gold to the glass.

Islamic glass production declined in the 1500s. By this time, more glass was being made in Europe, notably in Venice.

Metalware

Not many metal items from the past have survived because metal rusts. Metal items were also often melted down to be reshaped into a new item when the original item was broken or went out of fashion. A number of metal items are recorded in books and paintings.

Metals and Inlay

In the Islamic world, the metals used to make household objects were commonly brass and steel, and sometimes bronze. Many things were made from metal, including lamps, candlesticks, basins, bowls, buckets, boxes, pen cases, pans, and burners for incense (substances burned to scent rooms). Gold and silver were the most valued metals. These precious metals were used to make jewelry, such as earrings and necklaces. They were also used to decorate and enrich other metal objects.

Muslim metalworkers were skilled at working with inlay. Inlay was a technique used to decorate inexpensive metal items such as brass pots. The method involved engraving a pattern into the brass, then inlaying gold, silver, or copper into the engraved design. The technique was known by other cultures, but Muslim metalworkers were especially good at it.

Left: This painted battle scene shows the metal armor and swords used by Muslim warriors.

Left: This bronze incense burner is in the shape of a lion. The piercings in the design let the incense escape into the room. This lion was made in Persia in around 1100.

Making Patterns

Metalworkers used inlay to create animal figures and patterns of arabesques and calligraphy, often covering the entire surface of an object. Black inlay was also used to add contrast to the designs. It was made of bitumen from tar, or of pitch from coniferous tree sap. Inlay pieces were valued as highly as if they were made entirely from precious metals.

Other methods of decorating metal objects included piercing and repoussé. Incense burners were often made with pierced patterns of holes that allowed the perfume inside to escape into the air. Repoussé is a hammering technique. The metal is struck hard from the back against a soft substance. This technique creates a raised pattern.

Armor and Weapons

Islamic swords, armor, and helmets were made of steel, a toughened form of iron. The metal was decorated with patterns of gold or silver inlay, gilding, jewels, or enameled designs in animal and leaf shapes. Some armor and weapons had calligraphy, with words from the Quran or from the holy prophets. Such words were thought to protect the owners of the items. Ceremonial arms and armor used for displays were especially richly decorated with gold and gemstones.

Carpets

Muslim rulers and wealthy citizens valued finely made carpets. Carpets were used to cover floors and cushions, divide a room, or serve as decoration. People who were nomads lived in tents and had little furniture. Carpets, along with their livestock, were often their most valuable possessions.

Below: This silk carpet with its intricate animal design was made in Persia in the 1500s.

Making Carpets

Nomads were used to pitching their tents on rocky ground. A carpet made living close to the ground more comfortable. Carpets were also used in worship. Muslims prayed while kneeling on the ground. At home, they used small carpets for this purpose. Larger carpets were provided in mosques to pray on.

Sheep's wool was the most common fiber used to make carpets. Carpets were also made with goat or camel hair, silk, and cotton. Fibers were dyed to make different colors. The most expensive carpets were made with gold, silver, or other metal threads. The Mughal, Safavid, and Ottoman rulers set up carpet workshops and turned carpetmaking into an industry. Carpets were traded to Europe, where they were highly valued. At first, Europeans used carpets mainly as wall hangings and to cover furniture. Only later, as carpets became more affordable, were they put down on floors.

Above: Carpets were often made by women working on looms at home.

Persian and Turkish

The two most famous styles of carpets in the Islamic world were Persian and Turkish. They were different in the way the threads were knotted and in their patterns. Persian carpets had flowing lines and flower patterns. Turkish carpets were more geometric in pattern, some with a central medallion or round pattern, others with starlike patterns. Islamic-style carpets were also made in Spain, Egypt, and India.

Carpet Styles

Carpets that are fluffy on the surface have a "pile" and are made by knotting small lengths of yarn into a backing. A *kilim* is a flat-weave rug, woven on a loom rather than knotted, which creates a carpet with a flat surface. The design is woven into the rug. A felt rug is made by matting moist yarn fibers together and compressing them.

Textiles and Leather

Textiles are any type of cloth or woven fabric. They are mainly used to make clothing, but are also valued for their beauty as objects. Textiles could be decorated and very expensive, and were important trade items in the Islamic world.

Below: This painting shows a man using a *duruneh*, a bowlike tool used to prepare cotton for making cloth.

Making Cloth

Fine clothing was a way to show a person's rank or status. Clothing made from an expensive fabric showed that the wearer was someone important or rich.

Colored or patterned cloth was made in three ways: by printing designs on the fabric; by embroidering with thread on top of the fabric; and by weaving into the fabric itself with colored threads of silk, wool, and cotton.

One type of early Islamic textile made during the Fatimid Dynasty had a large border decorated with kufic calligraphy. This calligraphy was either embroidered or woven. The calligraphy gave the name and titles of the ruler. It also told people when and where the cloth was made. Such cloth is known as a *tiraz*, from a Persian word meaning "embroidery."

Tiraz cloth was made in workshops run by the government and given by the ruler to members of his court. The cloth was much prized by those who wore it.

Imperial Luxuries

The Safavid Empire was famed for luxury silk cloth, brocade, and velvet. Shah Abbas set up workshops in Isfahan to make silk brocade. The Ottoman Empire also became famous for its rich fabrics woven with satin and metallic threads. Ottoman sultans owned gold and silver cloth, highly decorated satins, and velvets. Textiles from India were popular across the Islamic world and were traded to Europe. Indian workers wove fabrics from cotton fiber, silk from wild silk moths, and wool from mountain goats. Emperor Akbar set up textile factories in cities.

Leatherwork

Leather was one of the most useful materials, because it was hardwearing and could be worked in many different ways. Leather was used to make covers for books, items of clothing such as belts and bags, saddles and bridles for horses, armor and shields for soldiers, and coverings for walls and furniture.

Andalusia in Spain became a center of leather production. Cordovan leather, from the city of Córdoba, became famous. Leather could be stamped, tooled, and gilded to create beautiful patterned works of art.

The Silk Route

Silk from China was traded to the Middle East, India, and Europe along the Silk Route or Silk Road. This was not a single road, but a network of trails and routes used by merchants. Other goods, including gemstones, spices, precious metals, carpets, and textiles were also traded. Goods were traded several times along the route by merchants, as one trader rarely traveled the entire distance. Caravans with camels carried most of the goods. Merchants stopped at night at caravanserai along the route.

Left: The traditional method of dyeing leather is to soak it in huge stone vats full of dye. This tannery in Morocco, where animals' skins are prepared to make leather, has changed little over hundreds of years.

Books

From the time of the Quran, books were valued in Islamic society as lasting records of learning and achievements. Bookmaking needed such arts and skills as bookbinding, calligraphy, and painting.

The Demand for Books

Copies of the Quran, and famous works of literature and history, were the most popular books. Each text was copied by hand. Pictures were painted individually on to the pages. Some books were made by papersellers or by scribes. These people sold books in markets, and were sometimes hired to make a book for a rich person, mosque, or madrasa. Books were also made in royal workshops that employed skilled workers. A rich patron decided which book he wanted. He placed an order with the workshop. The workshop boss then planned out the pages, decided what to illustrate, and gave out work to artists and scribes.

Making a Book

The first books were made of natural materials such as animal skins, called vellum or parchment. They were also made of a paperlike material from reeds called papyrus. These materials were later replaced with paper made from linen and hemp rags. The rags were soaked in water, mashed to a pulp, and dried in rectangle molds. The paper could be sprinkled with gold, tinted with color, or marbled to create swirling color patterns. It was treated with a starchy liquid to make it smooth and ready for ink.

A scribe made his own reed pen, and his own ink from plants and minerals. He pressed lines into the paper to show him where to write the text. Then he copied the words, left spaces for illustrations. More than one painter worked on the pictures for a book. When they had finished, gilders and illuminators added final flourishes. They decorated the chapter headings or the frames on the pages, and made the front and end papers. Then each page was polished with a smooth stone or piece of glass.

Lastly, the pages were sewn and bound together as a book. Covers made of pasteboard with leather on top were joined to a leather spine. Bindings were decorated with leatherworking tools to make geometric or floral patterns. In the 1400s, Persian bookbinders used a mold to make a central medallion with surrounding arabesque patterns. In the 1500s, bookbindings became even more elaborate. Pasteboard covers replaced leather bindings during the 1800s.

Libraries

Islamic libraries were book collections as well as places where students came to study. In libraries, new books were created and old books translated. Libraries employed scribes to make copies of books. Important mosques and madrasas had their own libraries, as did scholars, government officials, and wealthy families. Rulers collected books and valued them greatly. They gave books as gifts to other rulers and also set up public libraries.

Left: A scribe sits on the floor to work, as shown in a painting from a manuscript dated 1287.

Poetry and Prose

Beginning with spoken verses, poetry has a long tradition in the Islamic world. In Arabic, word patterns and complex rhythms and rhymes are used skillfully. These are not easily translated into other languages.

Forms of Poetry

Before Islam, Arab nomads told stories that were often poems handed down through generations. Such stories were often the first to be written down by Muslim scribes. At first, prose writing focused on the history of Islam. There were also biographies, or life stories, and books of instruction. Classic Persian and Indian tales were translated into Arabic. The Umayyad court at Damascus created a new form of epic literature to educate the growing numbers of government officials. The *Shahnameh* was one example.

The *Shahnameh*, or *Book of Kings*, is an epic poem. It was written in Persian around 1010 by the poet Abu'l Qasim Firdausi Tusi. It is written in 50,000 rhyming couplets and tells the story of the ancient kings of Persia from mythical beginnings to 651. The stories are about love, betrayal, and valor, as kings battle foreign enemies and supernatural creatures. It was one of the most popular books in Persia. The oldest copy was made during the Ilkhanid Dynasty of the 1200s. Other beautifully illustrated editions were made during the Timurid and Safavid dynasties after the 1400s.

Works in Prose

Early Arabic prose literature also followed specific styles, and it often used rhyme. The *maqamat* was a major work of literature. It first appeared in the 900s. It consisted of dramatic tales that poke fun at all levels of society. Al-Hamadhani wrote them down first, but later al-Hariri took them to higher levels. In one of his maqamat stories, al-Hariri uses only letters with no dots, which indicate pronunciation, and letters that do not connect to the next letter in a word. This shows his skill and mastery of language. Later, classic Persian and Indian tales were translated into Arabic, along with scientific works from Greek and other languages. Muslim writers also wrote histories, biographies, and travel books.

The Book of One Thousand and One Nights was a collection of tales from India, Persia, and the Middle East that were first written down in Iraq in the 900s. Antoine Galland translated the stories into French in the 1700s and, as *The Arabian Nights*, they became widely popular in Europe.

ماند درخت گل نو و در گلشن کشت ... عبدی کنت

مرگ ... ت ... میکذرکذ از خوشن ... ه ... وسی کنت

ستان کبه و در جبگ بیش ... ایشا ای ... بشنبده ... دنو ... زد که بود و جبگ ... پیش اپیکو ... نه بود و فز ... و سی ...

دستان جبگ بیش پیش ایشان کبت هرکر شنبده ... یو دنداش از ... حوش ... ب آمد آخرآم ... سه و سی ... کرد ... نه ...

و ... از و ... ر ... را ... یشرت ... با کبد کرسر ... برد مرجون ستان ... ده نبش ... ر ... منت شد ... و هربک ... کو کفت ... ده زر ... ورد و کی ... عضری

Above: The great Persian poet Abu'l Qasim Firdausi Tusi is shown here with court poets.

Rėligiȯuṣ Litėrᾳturė

The first form of Arabic prose writing were the *hadiths*, the record of the life, actions, and sayings of Muhammad. At first learned by heart, the hadiths were written down in the years after Muhammad's death in 632. Each hadith is written by someone who knew Muhammad personally, so each narrator's style comes through in the text. The hadiths are the second most holy book in Islam after the Quran. It was a source of Islamic moral and religious law. It was also used to create a history of early Islam.

Music and Dance

As Muslims conquered more lands, they learned about the music, dance, instruments, and theater of other cultures.

For and Against

The Islamic call to prayer is not considered a song or music by Muslims, even though it uses rhythm and tone changes made by the human voice. Reciting the Quran also uses rhythm, tone, and word shaping, and may be done in several different styles.

Religious leaders varied in their attitude to music and musical instruments, sometimes allowing them and at other times forbidding them. Those that forbade music felt that it turned people's minds away from religion and even encouraged them to sin. Others felt that music could bring people closer to God.

Musical instruments in the early Islamic world included various types of string instruments, drums, pipes, and flutes. The *oud*—from which the lute was developed—was the most important. Music was played, often by slaves, at feasts, weddings, and other celebrations.

The early Muslim caliphs frowned on music, but an Arabic style began under the Umayyad Caliphate or series of leaders.

Above: Musicians and dancers perform together in this simple painting.

Ibn Misjah is often called the father of Islamic music. He took from Persian and Byzantine music what he felt would work in Arab music. In the 700s, Yunus al-Katib put together the first collection of Islamic songs. He also wrote the first book of Islamic musical theory.

Islamic Music

Followers of the branch of Islam known as Sufism influenced Turkish music with their use of instruments, singing, poetry, and dance in their rituals. Military bands with drums, trumpets, and cymbals were used by the Egyptian Fatimids and later the Ottoman Turks.

Below: A lute has a hollow "soundbox" and a short "neck" or arm. Holes in the soundbox are covered with a grill. The strings are plucked with the fingers.

Song and Science

During the Abbasid Dynasty, people enjoyed music at the royal court and in wealthy homes. The oud, fiddles, zithers, drums, and wind instruments such as flutes and pipes were regularly played. Singers often accompanied the music. Men and women played musical instruments, and music was studied alongside philosophy, literature, and science. Music theory was developed and Greek writings on music were translated into Arabic.

Written Works

During the 900s, two important works on music were written. Al-Isfahani wrote *The Book of Songs*. This 24-book collection contained information about history, social life, and music from Islam's beginnings. It included musical theory as well as the words of popular songs. Al-Farabi wrote the *Grand Book on Music*. He wrote about theory, too, moving away from Ancient Greek ideas about music to a theory based on local musical practice. He also wrote about the theory of sound, tuning, and pitch.

Above: A musician plays soothing music on a harp while a Seljuk sultan, seated on his throne, greets leaders from a conquered land.

Music in Spain

Music was important in the rulers' courts of Islamic Spain. It was performed in palaces and other homes. Entertainment included instrumental music, songs, and dances, in which music from North Africa mingled with local music. The most noted musician and singer was Ali Ibn Nafi, known as *Ziryab* or "blackbird." He established a school of music and started new styles of performance and composition, which is the way of writing melodies. Seville was an important city for making musical instruments.

Shadow Plays

Shadow plays were a common type of entertainment. Puppeteers moved thin leather puppets on sticks in front of a light source, and their images appeared on a cloth screen to make a play. The plays were often comedies, making fun of the ruling class.

Theater and Dance

Actors, and performers such as dancers, worked as court entertainers for the caliphs and also performed for the rich in their homes. Unfortunately, few written scripts have ever been found. There were also traveling acting troupes who performed from memory or improvised. There were no public theater buildings, but performers entertained with musicians and dancers at feasts and celebrations. They performed in palaces and other homes, and put on shows in markets, inns, and on hillsides, working from wooden platforms.

Audiences stood or sat in a circle. They threw money at the performers if they liked the show.

Other popular forms of entertainment were shadow plays, marionettes or string puppets, hand puppets, and people dressed in costume as "hobby-horses." Shii Muslim actors performed *ta'ziya*, or religious plays, telling the story of the death in 680 of Muhammad's grandson, Husayn, at the Battle of Karbala.

Some Sufi mystics performed a ritual dance to seek perfection and glorify God. Known in the West as "whirling dervishes," they stood in a circle, then whirled faster in rhythm.

Left: Whirling dervishes spin in their ritual dance.

Painting

Paintings in the Islamic world were of religious and non-religious subjects. While in the West many paintings were large and designed to be hung on the wall, most Islamic painting works were small, detailed, book illustrations.

Scientific Illustration

Many early paintings were illustrations in manuscript books. Medical books showed drawings of the human body. In astronomy books and other scientific texts, pictures were added to illustrate the text. The paintings were often placed in the middle of the text to help explain the scientific ideas being described.

Pigments and Paints

Artists made their own paints from natural materials. The paints came from pigments, or colored powders made from ground up plants or minerals. Useful pigments included gold, silver, *lapis lazuli* (blue), malachite (green), and plants such as indigo (dark blue). The pigment was mixed with a liquid such as glue or albumen (egg white), which made the paint shiny. Gum arabic, from the sap of acacia trees, gave it a dull finish.

Below: This two-page miniature painting shows the magnificent funeral procession of the Mughal emperor Shah Jahan at Agra in 1666. The Taj Mahal is in the background.

Persian Miniature Painting

Under the Ilkhanid Dynasty in Persia, miniature painting flourished in the 1300s. The Ilkhanid rulers were Mongols and they brought Chinese art styles to Persia. Some of the best paintings of this period are from the *Shahnameh,* or *Book of Kings.* The paintings often take up most of a page. Objects such as battle flags are made to extend beyond the picture frame. The figures are sometimes cut off at the frame. This style gives the pictures an added sense of movement and life. Figures were painted from all angles, which made the paintings very lifelike. At this time, rulers began to sponsor, or pay, painters to work at royal courts.

The Timurid and Safavid rulers continued to encourage miniature painting. Ottoman miniatures were noted for their detail, such as in reproducing textile patterns. The Ottoman rulers also had artists make paintings that looked like maps, to show cities they had visited or had conquered in wars.

Muslim rulers hired artists to paint their portraits. They also liked large paintings of battles, and of musicians and dancers. These pictures were sometimes painted as frescoes on walls, or on palace ceilings. To make a fresco, paint was applied to fresh, damp plaster. Tombs, bathhouses, and mosques might also have wall paintings. Mosque paintings were only of floral or geometric patterns, and did not show people or animals.

Biographies

Ali Ibn Nafi

Born in or near Baghdad in the 800s, Ali Ibn Nafi later moved to Spain. A skillful musician and singer, he is said to have introduced the oud or lute to Spain, and gave it a fifth string. He was known as *Ziryab*, meaning "blackbird." Ali Ibn Nafi started a music school, with new styles of music and performance. He also invented a toothpaste and deodorant. He brought to Europe new food dishes and eating manners, such as tablecloths and drinking from glass, not metal, cups.

Al-Tabari

Al-Tabari was born in 839 and spent most of his life in Baghdad. He is known for two important works. *The History of Prophets and Kings* is a history of the world from creation to just before his own age. Where stories differ from accounts in Islamic history, he gives both versions so the reader can decide. His other work was *The Commentary on the Qur'an*, in which he analyzed the grammar of the text of the Quran and discussed different interpretations. He also gave his own opinions about the correct interpretation.

Al-Mutanabbi

The son of a poor water carrier, al-Mutanabbi is seen as one of the greatest Arab poets. He was so skilled in poetry at a young age that he was given a proper education. He began to write formal poems in praise of his rich patrons. After joining a royal court in Syria in 948, he wrote his best work. He gave the ode, or poem of praise, a more personal, freer style. His work is still regarded as among the best Arabic poetry.

Al-Biruni

Al-Biruni, writer of many encyclopedic works, lived from 973 to 1048. He is best known for writing about the culture of India in a work called *Verifying All That The Indians Recount, The Reasonable and The Unreasonable*. In it was everything al-Biruni could find about India's customs, science, religion, and literature. He also wrote the *Chronology of Ancient Nations* about the practice of old cultures that had been lost or were about to disappear. He also wrote on astronomy.

Omar Khayyam

Omar Khayyam, who lived from 1048 to 1131, was a Persian poet, astronomer, mathematician, and philosopher. His poetry was not seen as remarkable in his own time, but his verses became popular in the West in the 1800s after being freely translated into English by Edward

FitzGerald as *The Rubaiyat of Omar Khayyam*. This reintroduced his poetry in the East. His work is now widely known.

Ibn Tufail

In 1175, Ibn Tufail wrote *Hayy ibn Yaqdhan,* or *Alive, Son of the Vigilant,* the first-ever novel of ideas. It was known as *Philosophus Autodidactus* in Europe. The story is about a child raised on a desert island who lives alone for 50 years, and his self-education and philosophy. Some think it the first "coming of age" story. This novel influenced other writers, including Daniel Defoe, author of *Robinson Crusoe*. Ibn Tufail was also a philosopher and physician to an Almohad ruler in Spain.

Sinan

Sinan was the chief architect for the Ottoman court from 1538 to his death in 1588. He designed more than 450 buildings. He is renowned for spectacular domes on mosques. These domes have supporting walls pierced by windows that let in sunlight to brighten the interior. His greatest achievement was using eight pillars in an octagonal shape to support the large dome of the Selimiye Mosque, although he is most famous for his Suleymaniye Mosque. Both these buildings are in Turkey.

Above: Jalal al-Din Rumi lived from 1207 to 1273 and was a Sufi thinker and poet. His followers are known as Mevlevi, or whirling dervishes, because of their dancing.

Jalal Al-Din Rumi

Born in 1207, al-Din Rumi is described as the greatest Sufi mystic and Persian language poet. *The Collected Poetry of Shams,* contains mystical Persian verses. His *Masnavi* or *Spiritual Couplets* runs to more than 50,000 lines. Rumi's followers, the *Mevlevi,* became known in the West as the "whirling dervishes" for their whirling, mystical dancing in costume. Rumi himself was known to whirl to his own poetry.

Timelines

The Extent of the Early Islamic World

The Islamic Empire that began in Medina and Mecca during Muhammad's lifetime spread across the rest of the Arabian peninsula under Abu Bakr, the first caliph. Under the next two caliphs, Muslim armies broke out of the peninsula and took Syria and Palestine by 638, and Egypt and the Sasanian Empire of Persia in 642. In 711, Muslim armies invaded Spain and marched as far north as central France. By 750, Muslim power extended all the way to the borders of China and India. In later centuries, the Ottoman Empire conquered southeast Europe, while traders spread Islam into East Africa.

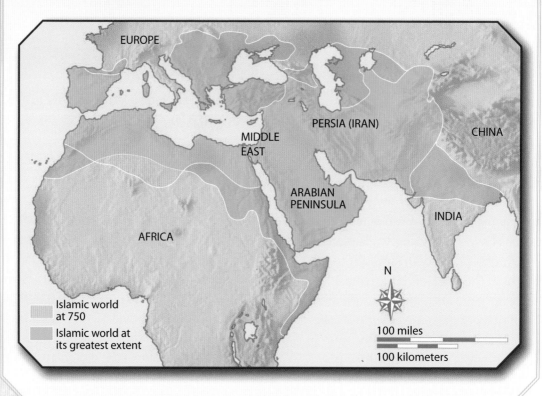

EUROPE

PERSIA (IRAN)

CHINA

MIDDLE EAST

ARABIAN PENINSULA

INDIA

AFRICA

N

Islamic world at 750

Islamic world at its greatest extent

100 miles

100 kilometers

Islamic World

570 Birth of Muhammad

632 Death of Muhammad

632–661 Rule of the first four caliphs

691 The al-Aqsa Mosque is built beside the Dome of the Rock in Jerusalem

670 Great Mosque is built in Kairouan, Tunisia

715 Umayyad Great Mosque is built in Damascus, Syria

749–1258 Abbasid Dynasty presides over a golden age, or blossoming, of Islamic culture

785 The building of the mosque of Córdoba in Spain begins

885–940 Life of Ibn Muqla, who made rules for calligraphic letters

897–967 Life of al-Isfahani, author of *The Book of Songs*

1010 Abu'l Qasim Firdausi Tusi writes the *Shahnameh*, or *Book of Kings*

1048–1131 Life of Omar Khayyam

1096–1099 First Crusade captures Jerusalem

1187 Saladin retakes Jerusalem

1207–1273 Life of Jalal al-Din Rumi, Sufi mystic and poet

1453 Ottoman sultan Mehmet II overthrows Byzantine Empire and takes Constantinople (Istanbul)

1492 Christians reconquer Granada

1551–1557 The Suleymaniye Mosque is built in Constantinople

1567–1574 The Selimiye Mosque is built in Edirne, Turkey

1632–1653 Taj Mahal is built in Agra, India

Rest of the World

476 Roman Empire collapses in Western Europe

526 Justinian expands Eastern Roman, later Byzantine, Empire

793 Vikings begin to attack England

800 Charlemagne of France crowned Holy Roman Emperor

1066 The Norman French conquer England

1163–1345 Notre Dame Cathedral built in Paris, France

1265–1321 Life of Dante Alighieri, poet and writer of the *Divine Comedy*

1387 Geoffrey Chaucer begins to write *The Canterbury Tales* in English

1400s Renaissance or rebirth of culture underway in Europe

1420–1436 Brunelleschi builds the dome of Florence Cathedral in Italy

1452–1519 Life of Leonardo da Vinci, painter, inventor, and sculptor

1455 Johannes Gutenberg prints the *Gutenberg Bible* on his new printing press

1492 Christopher Columbus sails to the New World (the Americas)

1475–1564 Life of Michelangelo Buonarroti, painter and sculptor

1519–1522 Ferdinand Magellan's crew completes first round-the-world sea voyage

1564–1616 Life of William Shakespeare, English playwright

1626 St. Peter's Basilica in Rome officially opens

Glossary

arabesque Stylized plant forms, such as leaves and flowers, used as decoration

Arabic The language of Arabia; something or someone of or from Arabia

Byzantine The empire or culture of Byzantium, based in Constantinople

caliphs Successors to Muhammad

calligraphy The art of decorative handwriting and lettering

caravans Groups of people and animals traveling together, usually transporting trade goods

ceramics Materials such as brick and porcelain made from minerals

cultures The arts, learning, and ways of life of peoples or civilizations

dynasty A series of rulers from the same family

idolatry The worship of idols, images of gods, or other supernatural beings

imams For Sunni Muslims, the people who lead prayer in mosques; for Shia, the leaders of Muslim communities

Islam The religion or faith based on God's messages to Muhammad

iwans Open spaces or halls with walls on three sides and the fourth side open

Kaaba A square building in Mecca; the holiest site in Islam

manuscripts Handwritten books or other pieces of writing

mihrab A niche in a wall of a mosque that marks the direction of Mecca

minarets Tall mosque towers used to call Muslims to prayer

minbar The platform used by an imam in a mosque to give his sermon

miniatures Small paintings in a book

Moorish Islamic North African culture

mosque A building used as a Muslim place of worship, or house of prayer

Mughal A Muslim empire in India

muqarnas Decorative tiers of niches

Muslims People who follow the faith of Islam

nomads People with no fixed home, who instead move from place to place

Ottoman A Turkish Muslim empire

pasteboard Papers glued together to make a thin board

Persian Something from the empire or culture of Persia, now known as Iran

pilgrimage A trip taken to a place that has religious importance

porcelain Pottery made from very fine clay

prophet A religious teacher who was inspired by God, as Muhammad was

qibla The wall in a mosque closest to Mecca

Quran Islam's holy book, containing the messages Muhammad said came from God

Sasanian The Persian empire and culture conquered by the Muslims in 642

scribes People skilled in writing and calligraphy

smiths Workers in metal

sultans The title of some Muslim rulers

textiles Fabrics made by weaving fibers

trade The buying and selling of goods

Further Information

Books

Barber, Nicola. *History in Art: Islamic Empires.* North Mankato, MN: Heinemann-Raintree, 2005.

Barber, Nicola. *Uncovering History: Everyday Life in the Ancient Arab & Islamic World.* North Mankato, MN: Smart Apple Media, 2005.

Barnard, Bryn. *The Genius of Islam: How Muslims Made the Modern World.* New York: Knopf Books for Young Readers, 2011.

Galloway, Priscilla, with Dawn Hunter. *Adventures on the Ancient Silk Road.* Toronto: Annick Press, 2009.

Kuiper, Kathleen, ed. *Islamic Art, Literature, and Culture.* New York: Rosen Education Service, 2009.

Macaulay, David. *Mosque.* New York: Houghton Mifflin/Walter Lorraine Books, 2003.

Major, John S., and Betty J. Belanus. *Caravan to America: Living Arts of the Silk Road.* Chicago: Cricket Books, 2002.

Reid, Struan. *The Silk and Spice Routes: Cultures and Civilizations.* Halifax, NS: Formac Publishing, 1994.

Roberts, J.M. *The Illustrated History of the World, Volume 4: The Age of Diverging Traditions.* New York: Oxford University Press, 2002.

Stone, Caroline. *Eyewitness Books: Islam.* New York: DK Children, 2005.

Websites

Islamic Art

http://salaam.co.uk/themeofthemonth/march02_index.php

Islamic Arts and Architecture

http://www.islamicart.com/index.html

Islamic Architectural History

http://www.islamic-architecture.info/A-HIST.htm

Museums with No Frontiers: Discover Islamic Art

http://www.discoverislamicart.org/index.php

The Islamic World to 1600: The Arts, Learning, and Knowledge.

http://www.ucalgary.ca/applied_history/tutor/islam/learning/

The Metropolitan Museum of Art: Islamic Art

http://www.metmuseum.org/toah/hi/te_index.asp?i=Islamic

Index

alphabet 8, 11
arabesque 4, 6, 9, 20, 21, 27, 32
arcades 12, 14, 17
arches 12, 13, 17
architecture 4, 12–13, 14, 20
armor 26, 27, 31
artists 4, 6, 20, 32, 40, 41

bathhouses 18, 19, 41
books 4, 6, 8, 26, 31, 32–33, 34, 35, 36, 37, 40

calligraphy and calligraphers 4, 6, 8–9, 10, 11, 12, 14, 21, 27, 30, 32
caravanserai 19, 31
carpets 4, 13, 28–29, 31
carvings 4, 20
ceramics 4, 8, 9, 22, 23, 25
clay 22, 23
coins 8, 9, 16
courtyard 12, 14, 17, 18

dome 12, 15, 18, 21, 43

earthenware 23

glass and glassware 4, 9, 23, 24–25, 32

glaze 22, 23
gold 6, 10, 14, 23, 25, 26, 27, 40

homes 16–17, 37, 38, 39

ink 10, 32
inlay 26, 27
ivory 20, 21
iwans 12, 14, 18

jewelry 8, 13, 26

lamps 22, 25, 26
leather 13, 30, 31, 32, 38
libraries 16, 33
lute 36, 37, 42

madrasa 18, 19, 32, 33
manuscripts 6, 13, 33, 40
markets 13, 32, 39
mausoleums 18, 19
metal 13, 26–27, 29
minarets 12, 14, 18
minbar 20
miniatures 6, 41
mosque 8, 11, 12, 13, 14, 15, 18, 21, 22, 25, 29, 32, 33, 41, 43
mudejar 20
Muhammad 4, 5, 8, 15, 39
muqarnas 5, 12

music 36–37, 38

paintings 8, 26, 33, 40, 41
palaces 16–17, 39
paper 10, 11, 32
papyrus 10, 32
parchment 10, 32
pens 10, 11, 32
Persia 27, 28, 34, 35, 41, 44
pigments 23, 40
plays 38, 39
poetry 8, 34, 42, 43
porcelain 22, 23
pottery 22–23

Quran 8, 10, 11, 20, 27, 32, 36, 42

Sasanian empire 4, 7
scribes 8, 10, 11, 32, 33, 34
script 10, 11
silk 10, 28, 29, 30, 31
silver 10, 23, 25, 26, 27, 29, 31, 40
Spain 5, 20, 29, 38, 43, 44

textiles 4, 6, 8, 30–31, 41
tiles 8, 12, 15, 22, 23

windows 12, 24, 43
windtowers 17
wood 8, 13, 20, 21, 39